One
devotional

One
devotional

ONE WORD, ONE VERSE, ONE THOUGHT
FOR ONE HUNDRED DAYS

SUSAN ALEXANDER YATES

Published by Susan Alexander Yates
www.susanalexanderyates.com

Printed in the United States of America

Cover Design by Darlene Schacht
Interior Design by Roseanna White Designs

ISBN 978-1981340026

You can find out more about Susan and her books by visiting: www.susanalexanderyates.com where you can sign up on her website to receive a twice weekly "One Word" email.

TABLE OF CONTENTS

INTRODUCTION

A few years ago I realized that often when I woke up and began to think about my day I became discouraged. There was no prevailing reason why, simply a feeling of dread followed by guilt for feeling this way.

Parents of young children don't have the luxury of thinking before they get out of bed. More likely there's some little foot kicking them or a big voice screaming for them. But some of us don't have kids. Others have reached the season when we do have a few minutes to awaken and the time to contemplate. It can be a moment of rejoicing or a moment of feeling blue. It depends upon our focus. Lying in bed that morning I realized I needed to adjust my attitude, to shift from thinking about *how I felt* about my day to focusing on God. Paul tells us in Romans 12:2,

"Do not be conformed to this world, but be transformed by the renewal of your mind, that by testing you may discern what is the will of God, what is good and acceptable and perfect."

It was a different kind of wake-up call for me.

In the gospel of John there is a scene in which Jesus is talking with His disciples as He tries to prepare them for His death. He says, "But the Helper, the Holy Spirit, whom the Father will send in my name, he will teach you all things and bring to your remembrance all that I have said to you" (John 14:26).

To stop my habit of thinking negatively as I woke up I began to ask the Holy Spirit to *remind me* of one character trait of God the Father or of His Son that I could meditate on that day. I lay still until one became clear to me.

I remember the first day I did this, the trait that I thought of was *He is a God who **rescues*** (Psalm 18:19, Psalm 91:14-16). Hopping out of bed with more joy than usual I went to get a cup of tea when my phone rang. A friend on the line burst into tears, "Susan," she exclaimed, "I'm having so much trouble with my teenage son. I feel like he needs to be rescued." Can you imagine the joy that flooded my heart? It was as if the Holy Spirit placed an exclamation point over His leading.

On another day the character trait was *He is a God who **lavishes*** (Ephesians 1:8). As I thought about God lavishing His love on me I realized how radical that was. Too often I act as if He parcels out his love - trickle by trickle, drip by drip, definitely sparingly, without waste. Oh no! He lavishes. Contemplating this fact changed my entire day!

One morning I awoke paralyzed with indecision. There was a decision I had to make and I did not know what to do. I didn't trust my instincts. I needed Him to lead, to direct, to speak. But would He? I turned in my regular reading to Psalm 29, and saw repeatedly the phrase: *the voice of the Lord*. Yes. He would speak in His time in His way. Sometimes His timing seems slow. I am impatient. But I can have the assurance that He will **speak.**

For many years I have continued this habit. Sometimes I forget and then slowly the morning blues return. I realize I need to resume my habit. Psalm 90:14 states,

"Satisfy us in the morning with your steadfast love that we may rejoice and be glad all our days." This small practice has changed my attitude and enabled me to focus more on Him throughout each day.

This little devotional will encourage you to begin a daily habit of focusing on one character trait of our amazing God. It is so easy for our lives to become *about me and my stuff.* When this happens we lose perspective and our joy begins to evaporate. God delights in revealing himself to us. If we begin to walk through each day focusing on Him and His character we will gain a healthier perspective on *our stuff*.

In this book I refer to God the Father, God the Son—Jesus—and God, the Holy Spirit. I may not make clear distinctions as they are three in one. I will leave the theological explanations of the Trinity to others.

In his "High Priestly Prayer" Jesus captures this sense of oneness as he prays for us,

"I do not ask for these only (*the disciples*) but also for those who will believe in me through their word (*that's you and me*), that they may all be one, just as you Father are in me and I in you, that they also may be in us, so that the world may believe that you have sent me." (John 17: 20-21, emphasis mine)

It is truly amazing to contemplate that at this very moment Jesus is in heaven sitting at the right hand of the Father praying for you and for me. (Hebrews 7:25, Romans 8:34)

I encourage you to use this book for yourself, but also for your family. Choose a character trait of God or Jesus or the Holy Spirit and share it at breakfast. Children can have an assigned day to choose a trait. Keep a bible handy so you can mark the reference. There is a strong message in seeing His word on paper and underlining it. By doing this, your kids will learn how powerful and practical the word of God is. Occasionally I have used several words to more clearly emphasize one trait.

You can use the extra space for jotting down the ways in which you might apply this verse to your lives today. Or you might write out a prayer for yourselves or someone else. I hope the pages in your devotional will become all marked up, full of your own notes of God's work in your life. A messy book is a meaningful book.

My prayer is that this little book would spur you on to ask God to reveal to you a trait of His that meets your needs today. As you discover more and more of Him you will be amazed by His overflowing abundance and bigness.

To My Sister Fran

Whose love for God's word
is a great encouragement to me.
I love you, Sis.

One Word

KNOWS

ONE VERSE

"O Lord, you have searched me
and known me."

~ Psalm 139:1

ONE THOUGHT

God knows me even better than I know
myself. He knows what I need today.
He knows where I am struggling and
He understands. Oh, the joy of being
totally known and, in spite of that, still
completely and thoroughly loved.

One Word

GENEROUS

One Verse

"If any of you lacks wisdom,
let him ask God who gives
generously to all without reproach,
and it will be given him."

~ James 1:5

One Thought

Too often I act as if God parcels out his
wisdom to me. I forget that He longs to
be generous. He wants me to have his
generous wisdom even more than I do
and He will give it to me in His time and
in His way. I can count on Him to give
me wisdom about _____.

One Word

DELIGHTS

One Verse

"Great is the Lord who delights in the
welfare of his servant"

~ Psalm 35:27b

One Thought

It's easy to wonder, *how can anyone
delight in me*? I don't even like myself
today. But my heavenly Father is
delighting in me and in you at this very
moment and He will continue to do so
throughout this day. He delights in us
simply because we are HIS.

One Word

PROVIDES

One Verse

"As for the rich in this present age, charge them not to be haughty, nor to set their hopes on the uncertainty of riches, but on God who richly provides us with everything to enjoy."

~ 1 Timothy 6:17b

One Thought

God is providing right now—for me, for my child, for my friend—in ways that I do not even know. He is already providing for the future even before it gets here.

One Word

HEARS

One Verse

"I love the Lord for he has heard my
voice and my pleas for mercy."

~ Psalm 116:1

One Thought

Sometimes I don't feel like anyone hears
me— even you, God. But I am wrong.
Even if no one else hears me, YOU do.
You hear my cries and you hear my
silent thoughts. And you hear me with
joy! At this very moment you hear me!

One Word

EQUIPS

One Verse

"Now may the God of peace, brought again from the dead our Lord Jesus Christ, the great shepherd of the sheep, by the blood of the eternal covenant, equip you with everything good that you may do his will, working in us that which is pleasing in his sight through Jesus Christ to whom be the glory forever and ever amen."

~ Hebrews 13:20-21

One Thought

Too often I think you might be calling me to do something but I panic because I don't think I can do it. I forget that you will equip me for what you have called me to do, from raising a difficult child to completing a challenging project.

One Word

RULES

One Verse

"The Lord has established his throne
in the heavens, and his kingdom rules
over all."

~ Psalm 103:19

One Thought

When it seems like everything is falling
apart I can count on the fact that you are
still in charge. Some days I need to say
over and over, "You are still in charge."

One Word

UNDERSTANDS

One Verse

"Great is our Lord and abundant in power; his understanding is beyond measure."

~ Psalm 147:5

One Thought

When no one else can understand me or my situation, you do, completely O Lord.

One Word

LIGHT

ONE VERSE

"God is light and in him
there is no darkness at all."

~ 1 John 1:5

ONE THOUGHT

Even if there is darkness around there is
no darkness in you. You are light. Help
me to rest today with this picture of
your strong light.

One Word

_____

WORKS

ONE VERSE

"The Lord works righteousness and
justice for all who are oppressed."

~ Psalm 103:6

ONE THOUGHT

Even when I can't see it, you are working
while I'm waiting.

One Word

LAVISHES

ONE VERSE

"In him we have redemption through
his blood, the forgiveness of trespasses,
according to the riches of his grace
which he lavished upon us."

~ Ephesians 1:8

ONE THOUGHT

Too often I act as if you measure out
your love in small increments. How
wrong I am! You are lavishing your love
on me and on _____ right at this very
moment.

One Word

RESCUES

One Verse

"He brought me out into a broad place; he rescued me because he delighted in me"

~ Psalm 18:19

One Thought

You long to rescue me, my relative, my child, my friend. Please be doing this for _____ today.

One Word

MAKES
KNOWN

ONE VERSE

"The friendship of the Lord is for those
who fear Him; and he makes known
to them his covenant."

~ Psalm 25:14

ONE THOUGHT

You do make known your will, in your
time, in your way. You remind me of this
in creation. Reassure me of this when I
have to wait.

One Word

PRESENCE

ONE VERSE

"My Presence will go with you
and I will give you rest."

~ Exodus 33:14

ONE THOUGHT

Thank you that your presence is with
me. You never leave me. Right at this
moment I am surrounded by your
presence.

One Word

_____

FORGIVES

ONE VERSE

"If we confess our sins, he is faithful
and just to forgive us our sins and to
cleanse us from all unrighteousness."

~ 1 John 1:9

ONE THOUGHT

Even when I can't forgive myself or
someone else, you do, and you will
enable me to also.

One Word

INTERCEDES

One Verse

"And he who searches hearts knows what is the mind of the Spirit because the Spirit intercedes for the saints according to the will of God."

~ Romans 8:27

One Thought

Jesus, how amazing to think that right now you are at the right hand of the Father interceding for me, for my child, for my friend, for _____. It isn't all up to me to pray for this person. You - my Savior, my King - are interceding right now!

One Word

CREATES
NEW THINGS

ONE VERSE

"Remember not the former things,
nor consider the things of old.
Behold, I am doing a new thing;
now it springs forth, do you not perceive it?
I will make a way in the wilderness
and rivers in the desert."

~ Isaiah 43:18-19

ONE THOUGHT

Father, sometimes I get tired of me. Today, I ask you to do something *new* within me. I long to *see YOU* in new ways. Today I ask that you would give me an expectant heart that looks to you for *new things* in this season.

One Word

FILLS

ONE VERSE

"May the God of hope fill you with all joy and peace in believing so that by the power of the Holy Spirit you may abound in hope."

~ Romans 15:13

ONE THOUGHT

Lord, I'm empty. Please fill me today with your Holy Spirit.

One Word

TEMPTED

One Verse

"For because he himself has suffered
when tempted, he is able to help those
who are being tempted."

~ Hebrews 2:18

One Thought

Jesus, you understand my temptation
because you were tempted in every way
that I am or ever will be. During your
40 days in the wilderness you suffered
temptation. You alone know this pain
and you will deliver me if I let you.

One Word

HOLDS

ONE VERSE

"Nevertheless, I am continually with
you; you hold my right hand."

~ Psalm 73:23

ONE THOUGHT

Dear God, help me to remember all day
today that you are holding my hand.
You never let go.

One Word

SATISFIES

ONE VERSE

"Praise the Lord oh my soul...who
satisfies your desires with good so that
your youth is renewed like the eagle's"

~ Psalm 103:5

ONE THOUGHT

Lord, sometimes when I look at the
future it feels empty and fearful. Thank
you for reminding me that you will
satisfy me and renew me. You have a
new purpose for me.

One Word

_____

ADOPTION

One Verse

"In love, he predestined us for adoption
as sons through Jesus Christ according
to the purpose of his will."

~ Ephesians 1:5

One Thought

Father, you are the God of adoption.
You adopted me. Through Jesus
I am now your child. Chosen,
accepted, loved forever. Help
_____ to realize how special it is to be
adopted.

One Word

HIDES ME

One Verse

"Keep me as the apple of your eye;
hide me in the shadow of your wings."

~ Psalm 17:8

One Thought

Father, I love the image of your hiding
me in the shadow of your wings. You
have me covered. You have my back
covered. You are protecting me, my
child, my friend today. Help me to rest
in the assurance that I am hidden in you.

One Word

NEAR

One Verse

"Draw near to God,
and he will draw near to you."

~ James 4:8

One Thought

You, O Lord, are the God who comes
near, who is near. You are not far away.
You are here with me, with _____ at
this very moment

One Word

GOOD
SHEPHERD

One Verse

"I am the good shepherd. The good
shepherd lays down his life for the sheep."

~ John 10:11

One Thought

Lord, how easy it is to forget that you
are my Good Shepherd. You LOVE me.
You will lead me. You are my child's
shepherd, my spouse's shepherd. Help
me dwell on this as I walk through this
day...Jesus, my good shepherd.

One Word

_____

ANSWERS

One Verse

"Out of my distress I called on the Lord,
the Lord answered me and set me free."

~ Psalm 118:5

One Thought

Thank you Father that you always answer my prayer—sometimes with a "yes," other times with a "no" and occasionally in the silence you are saying "wait." Your answer is always motivated by your personal love for me. You are the only one with the whole picture. And you know the very best answer. You will set me free.

One Word

IS

ADVOCATING

One Verse

"My little children, I am writing these things to you so that you may not sin. But if anyone does sin, we have an advocate with the Father, Jesus Christ the righteous."

~ 1 John 2:1

One Thought

How much I need to know that you, Jesus, are for me. You represent me. You are saying to our Father, "Forgive this child. I died with her sin on my shoulders." Oh what comfort to know that you are for me, for my child, for my friend. And you are my advocate when I face those who do not believe.

One Word

MAN OF SORROWS

One Verse

"He was despised and rejected by men;
a man of sorrows,
and acquainted with grief..."

~ Isaiah 53:3

One Thought

Jesus, you, more than anyone else, know grief. The deep piercing agony of sorrow. Father, comfort _____ with the assurance that you personally understand their grief. You too ache with them.

One Word

CARRIES

ONE VERSE

"He will tend his flock like a shepherd;
he will gather the lambs in his arms;
he will carry them in his bosom,
and gently lead those that are with young."

~ Isaiah 40:11

ONE THOUGHT

Father, thank you for this image of your carrying me, (my child, etc.). Help me to keep this image in the front of my brain as I walk through this day. You are carrying me.

One Word

GIVES LIGHT

ONE VERSE

"The unfolding of your words gives light;
it imparts understanding to the simple."

~ Psalm 119:130

ONE THOUGHT

Father, sometimes I'm in the dark about
what to do, what to say. Thank you that
you give light. Give me a hunger to be
in your word today, for your word will
give me light on my situation.

One Word

_____

CLEANSES

One Verse

"If we confess our sins, he is faithful
and just to forgive us our sins and to
cleanse us from all unrighteousness."

~ 1 John 1:9

One Thought

Lord, you are the God who cleanses.
You don't just forgive. You cleanse. And
THAT is an amazing thing to think
about today. I can be completely clean.

One Word

KINDNESS

ONE VERSE

"But when the goodness and loving kindness of God our Savior appeared, he saved us, not because of works done by us in righteousness, but according to his own mercy, by the washing of regeneration and renewal of the Holy Spirit."

~ Titus 3:4-5

ONE THOUGHT

It's so easy for me to focus on my unworthiness but today I want to focus on your kindness. Your loving kindness which is always reaching out towards me. Help me to notice and to receive your kindnesses today.

One Word

FAITHFUL

One Verse

"Know therefore that the Lord your God is
God, the faithful God who keeps covenant
and steadfast love with those who love
him and keep his commandments,
to a thousand generations."

~ Deuteronomy 7:9

One Thought

In this world things aren't fair or just. So
much is wrong but you are in the midst
of it all and you, Oh Lord, will remain
faithful to the end. I can count on you.

One Word

POURS OUT

.

ONE VERSE

"And thereby put me to the test, says the Lord of hosts, if I will not open the windows of heaven for you and pour down for you a blessing until there is no more need."

~ Malachi 3:10b

ONE THOUGHT

Too often I live with the false assumption that your answer will be "can't do it" or something else negative. But you are a Father who loves to say "yes." Help me live today with the vision that you love to pour out blessing.

One Word

SAVES

One Verse

"The saying is trustworthy and deserving of full acceptance, that Christ Jesus came into the world to save sinners, of whom I am the foremost."

~ 1 Timothy 1:15

One Thought

Father, I am a sinner. Thank you for saving me once and for all. Help _____ to come to realize that you want to save him (or her) as well. Your nature is to SAVE. Your love compels it. You cannot help it. You sent Jesus to redeem each one of us.

One Word

INSTRUCTOR

ONE VERSE

"I will instruct you and teach you
in the way you should go; I will counsel
you with my eye upon you."

~ Psalm 32:8

ONE THOUGHT

When I don't know which way to go,
where to turn, how to decide, what
to decide, you, God, will instruct me.
Enable me to wait for your instruction.

One Word

SURROUNDS

One Verse

"Many are the sorrows of the wicked,
but steadfast love surrounds the one
who trusts in the Lord."

~ Psalm 32:10

One Thought

Father, as I walk through today, help me
to do so with a sense of being surrounded
by a thick fog of your unfailing love. I ask
this also for _____.

One Word

STEADFAST
LOVE

One Verse

"Let your steadfast love, O Lord, be upon us, even as we hope in you."

~ Psalm 33:22

One Thought

Father, your love never ever fails or runs out. No matter what I do. On the other hand, my love fails. And so does that of every human. Only your love does not. Keep your steadfast love as the song in my heart today.

One Word

ESTABLISHES
MY STEPS

ONE VERSE

"The heart of man plans his way,
but the Lord establishes his steps."

~ Proverbs 16:9

ONE THOUGHT

It gives me great security to know that you are establishing my steps. When I look back on my life I see your hand all over it, even when I did not realize it. And now, you are establishing my future steps even though they seem blurry to me at the moment.

One Word

FOUNDER
AND
PERFECTER

ONE VERSE

"...let us run with endurance the race
that is set before us, looking to Jesus,
the founder and perfecter of our faith."

~ Hebrews 12:1-2

ONE THOUGHT

You are the author of my faith. You
began it, Father. It is yours. I ask you
to be perfecting it. Thank you that even
this isn't up to me. My part is to fix my
eyes on you and let you do your work
within me.

One Word

SUPPLIES

One Verse

"And my God will supply every need
of yours according to his riches
in glory in Christ Jesus."

~ Philippians 4:19

One Thought

Father, thank you that you will supply
all of my needs, even those I don't know
about yet. You are abundantly rich. I can
count on you.

One Word

FORSAKEN

ONE VERSE

"My God, my God,
why have you forsaken me?"

~ Matthew 27:46

ONE THOUGHT

Lord Jesus, I think about the fact that you were forsaken. You were completely forsaken by God the Father in my place so that I would never be forsaken by Him. You understand at the deepest level what it means to be left alone, betrayed, forsaken.

One Word

LOVED

One Verse

"As the Father has loved me, so have I
loved you. Abide in my love."

~ John 15:9

One Thought

Jesus, you were loved with a perfect love
by Father God and now you are loving
me with this same love. Help me (my
friend, my child) to count on this perfect
love today. I want to walk through these
hours whispering, *I am loved.*

One Word

REIGNS

ONE VERSE

"Let the heavens be glad,
and let the earth rejoice,
and let them say among the nations,
'The Lord reigns!'"

~ 1 Chronicles 16:31

ONE THOUGHT

Father, no matter how crazy life is, you still reign. Nothing changes this. You reign, period. Dwelling on this truth makes me feel safe and secure. It provides perspective for my small world.

One Word

RICH IN
MERCY

One Verse

"But God, being rich in mercy,
because of the great love with which he
loved us, even when we were dead in
our trespasses, made us alive together
with Christ—by grace
you have been saved—"

~ Ephesians 2:4-5

One Thought

Father, how easily I forget that you are
rich in mercy, giving and doing for me
what I don't deserve and then forgiving
me again and again. Please help _____ to
recognize today that you are rich in
mercy towards him or her. Your mercy
never runs out.

One Word

PROMISE
GIVER

One Verse

"...by which he has granted to us
his precious and very great promises,
so that through them you may become
partakers of the divine nature..."

~ 2 Peter 1:4

One Thought

Thank you Lord that you have not left us to guess what you are like and how you want us to live. In your scriptures you have given us promises (it is said there are over 3000 in the New Testament alone) for us to take you up on. I want to learn your promises and live each day taking you up on them.

One Word

LOVE AND
FAITHFULNESS

One Verse

"God will send out his steadfast love
and his faithfulness!"

~ Psalm 57:3b

One Thought

Yours is an active, energizing love, and always faithful. It is not sedentary. You are sending love and faithfulness to me at this moment. May I dwell on these "twins" of love and faithfulness throughout this day.

One Word

TEMPTED

One Verse

"Then Jesus was led up by the Spirit
into the wilderness to be
tempted by the devil."

~ Matthew 4:1

One Thought

Jesus, even you were tempted. You understand the strong pull of every temptation we will face. You know the agony. For you, it must have been even more excruciating because you were completely pure, without sin. When I am tempted you comfort me and deliver me.

One Word

_____

ALIVE AND ACTIVE WORD

One Verse

"For the word of God is living and
active, sharper than any two-edged
sword, piercing to the division of soul
and of spirit, of joints and of marrow,
and discerning the thoughts
and intentions of the heart."

~ Hebrews 4:12

One Thought

Thank you, Father, that your word is
alive and active. It is not merely a sweet
saying or a nice piece of wisdom. It is
powerful and it is at work within me
and within your world. Give to me and
to those I love a hunger to know it, a
desire to obey it, and the courage to
proclaim it. Throughout this day, I want
to think about things in your word.

One Word

HIGH PRIEST

ONE VERSE

"For we do not have a high priest
who is unable to sympathize with our
weaknesses, but one who in every
respect has been tempted as we are,
yet without sin."

~ Hebrews 4:15

ONE THOUGHT

Jesus, only you can completely
understand my temptations, my
weaknesses, my feelings. You alone
"get me" because you have experienced
everything I have and will. Help me
to remember this when I feel alone.
Thank you for whispering today, "I
understand."

One Word

PEACE

ONE VERSE

"On the evening of that day, the first day of the week, the doors being locked where the disciples were for fear of the Jews, Jesus came and stood among them and said to them, 'Peace be with you.'"

~ John 20:19

ONE THOUGHT

Jesus, you are the Prince of Peace. You knew that what the frightened disciples needed most was a sense of peace, your peace. Jesus, this is what we too need today. Thank you that you are PEACE. Help _____ to rest in the awareness of your peace today.

One Word

DOES NOT
LIE

One Verse

"...in hope of eternal life, which God,
who never lies, promised
before the ages began."

~ Titus 1:2

One Thought

Father, how grateful I am that there is one thing you cannot do. You cannot lie. In a world that is often run on lies, you always speak the truth. For you are truth personified. Thank you that I can always count on you.

One Word

REMINDS

ONE VERSE

"But the Helper, the Holy Spirit, whom
the Father will send in my name, he will
teach you all things and bring to your
remembrance all that I have said to you."

~ John 14:26

ONE THOUGHT

Father, thank you that one of the jobs of
the Holy Spirit is to remind us of what
you have taught us. I so easily forget
who you are, what you've done, and the
things you have shown me. I ask you
today to remind me of your character
traits and of the ways in which you
have worked.

One Word

MAN OF WAR

One Verse

"The Lord is a man of war;
the Lord is his name."

~ Exodus 15:3

One Thought

Lord, it is good for me to be reminded that you are a warrior. You are not a wimp, or a pushover, or weak. You are mighty. You fight for me. You defend me. You have my back. You are *for me.*

One Word

STABILITY

ONE VERSE

"...and he will be the stability of your
times, abundance of salvation, wisdom,
and knowledge; the fear of the
Lord is Zion's treasure."

~ Isaiah 33:6

ONE THOUGHT

Father, there's not much that is sure,
stable, unmoving, and true in our
culture. However, you, O Lord, are our
Sure Foundation. I pray that all of my
kids and grandkids and those to come
will live in this truth. *The Church's one
foundation is Jesus Christ her Lord. (a
hymn from the 1800's, Samuel Stone &
Samuel Wesley).*

One Word

GUIDES

One Verse

"When the Spirit of truth comes, he will guide you into all the truth."

~ John 16:13

One Thought

Father, thank you for sending your Holy Spirit to guide me into truth. Today I need guidance about _____. I ask your Holy Spirit to guide me into truth.

One Word

_____

STRONGHOLD

ONE VERSE

"The Lord is a stronghold for the
oppressed,
a stronghold in times of trouble."

~ Psalm 9:9

ONE THOUGHT

Father, thank you that you are my
stronghold. So often I forget that and
I feel like running away. Help me and
help _____ to run to you today. Your
refuge always provides a stronghold in
times of trouble.

One Word

KINGDOM

ONE VERSE

"Pray then like this:
'Our Father in heaven, hallowed be
your name. Your kingdom come...' "

~ Matthew 6:9-10

ONE THOUGHT

Father, you are a "Kingdom God." Sometimes on earth it's easy to feel marginalized, belittled, and small because of our faith. It is comforting to remember that your kingdom alone will ultimately be victorious. Your kingdom is pure, good, holy, and lasting.

One Word

WORKS

One Verse

"For it is God who works in you, both to will and to work for his good pleasure."

~ Philippians 2:13

One Thought

Father, thank you that you are the one working within me, even if I don't see it and can't feel it. You are still at work. And you are at work in my child's life as well.

One Word

WISDOM

One Verse

"It is he who made the earth by his power, who established the world by his wisdom, and by his understanding stretched out the heavens."

~ Jeremiah 10:12

One Thought

Father God, you are wisdom—complete wisdom. I lack wisdom and I know you desire to fill my "lacks." Please give me wisdom about ____. Reassure me that you will give me wisdom when I need it. Too often I want it *now*.

One Word

JUSTICE

One Verse

"For the Lord is a God of justice;
blessed are all those who wait for him."

~ Isaiah 30:18b

One Thought

Father, sometimes it seems that evil wins and there is no justice. But you, oh Lord, are the God of Justice. In your time, in your way, we will see you bring justice. Thank you for this assurance as we wait.

One Word

_____

OVERCOMER

One Verse

"I have said these things to you, that in
me you may have peace. In the world
you will have tribulation. But take
heart; I have overcome the world."

~ John 16:33

One Thought

Father, it is *helpful* to know that we
shouldn't be surprised by trouble in
this world. But it is *comforting* to know
you have and will overcome whatever
happens here.

One Word

WITH YOU

One Verse

"Have I not commanded you? Be
strong and courageous. Do not be
frightened, and do not be dismayed,
for the Lord your God is with you
wherever you go."

~ Joshua 1:9

One Thought

Father, you are a "*with me*" God. Just as
you promised Joshua, you promise us.
Please remind ____ that you are with her
or him today. Help me walk through this
day hearing you say, "I am with you."

One Word

MAJESTIC

One Verse

"O Lord, our Lord, how majestic is your name in all the earth! You have set your glory above the heavens."

~ Psalm 8:1

One Thought

My Father and my Lord, there are so many unpleasant, sad, depressing things I could think on today. Instead, I want to dwell on your wonderful majesty and contemplate what it means.

One Word

TRUE VINE

One Verse

"I am the true vine,
and my Father is the vinedresser."

~ John 15:1

One Thought

Jesus, many today say there is no one
who is reliable. But you say you are
the true vine. I can dwell in you and be
secure and fruitful. You will provide all
I need. Help me to rest in this security
today.

One Word

SUFFICIENT

ONE VERSE

"But he said to me, 'My grace is
sufficient for you, for my power is
made perfect in weakness'."

~ 2 Corinthians 12:9

ONE THOUGHT

Jesus, I am weak and I think I need
so much. But your grace, oh Lord, is
sufficient for me. Teach me today how
to walk in this truth, to let your grace
overwhelm my weaknesses.

One Word

MYSTERY

One Verse

"To them God chose to make known how great among the Gentiles are the riches of the glory of this mystery, which is Christ in you, the hope of glory."

~ Colossians 1:27

One Thought

You are a God of mystery. It's a glorious mystery. I can't explain you even though sometimes I want to. Your mystery is a part of what makes you so much greater than man. Thank you that you, with all of your glorious mystery, have chosen to dwell in me.

One Word

JOY

ONE VERSE

"And do not be grieved,
for the joy of the Lord is your strength."

~ Nehemiah 8:10

ONE THOUGHT

Father, you are the God of JOY. Your joy is my strength. Help me, help _____ to be assured of your joy today in some particular way.

One Word

FIGHTS

One Verse

"The Lord will fight for you,
and you have only to be silent."

~ Exodus 14:14

One Thought

Thank you, Lord, that as you fought
for Moses you will fight for me, for my
child. I need to be still and rest in this
knowledge. You've got my back and my
child's back.

One Word

IMMEASURABLE RICHES

ONE VERSE

"...so that in the coming ages he might show the immeasurable riches of his grace in kindness toward us in Christ Jesus."

~ Ephesians 2:7

ONE THOUGHT

Father, today I long to dwell on your riches rather than my wants and my needs. Recall to my mind your riches and help these thoughts of you to be in the forefront of my thinking today.

One Word

EVERY

One Verse

"Blessed be the God and Father of our
Lord Jesus Christ, who has blessed us
in Christ with every spiritual blessing
in the heavenly places."

~ Ephesians 1:3

One Thought

Father, that word *every* is power packed.
Even though I feel so many "lacks",
the truth is I lack nothing. You have
given me all. Help me today to dwell
on this and to grow into recognizing
the "everys" which you have already
provided in Jesus.

One Word

STIRS UP

ONE VERSE

"Now in the first year of Cyrus king
of Persia, that the word of the Lord
by the mouth of Jeremiah might be
fulfilled, the Lord stirred up the spirit
of Cyrus king of Persia, so that he
made a proclamation throughout all his
kingdom and also put it in writing."

~ 2 Chronicles 36:22

ONE THOUGHT

Father, you are a God who stirs up
the hearts—of those who know you
and of those who don't acknowledge
you. Please move the heart of
____. Thank you for your supernatural
power that accomplishes this according
to your will for what is best.

One Word

CALLS

One Verse

"I will give you the treasures of
darkness and the hoards in secret
places, that you may know that it is I,
the Lord, the God of Israel, who call
you by your name."

~ Isaiah 45:3

One Thought

Lord, not only did you call Cyrus by
name, you call me by name and you
are calling _____ by name. Oh, the
sweet, personal "love touch" of being
summoned by my name. Today I want
to walk in this truth: *You call me.*

One Word

JEALOUS

ONE VERSE

"For you shall worship no other god,
for the Lord, whose name is Jealous, is
a jealous God."

~ Exodus 34:14

ONE THOUGHT

Lord you are jealous for me, for _____.
It is a "love jealousy." So great is your
love that you want me completely for
yourself. To be wanted this much is
hard to take in. May I walk today with
the thought: *You want me.*

One Word

ALPHA AND OMEGA

ONE VERSE

"I am the Alpha and the Omega," says
the Lord God, "who is and who was
and who is to come, the Almighty."

~ Revelation 1:8

ONE THOUGHT

Lord, you are *it*. There never has been
anyone or anything else, nor will there
ever be. You are the best—my Almighty.
How reassuring, how comforting, how
secure!

One Word

OIL OF JOY

One Verse

"...Therefore your God has anointed
you with the oil of gladness beyond
your companions."

~ Hebrews 1:9

One Thought

Father, you choose to anoint your
children with the oil of gladness. I ask
you to anoint _____ with gladness and
joy today.

One Word

HATED

One Verse

"If the world hates you, know that it
has hated me before it hated you."

~ John 15:18

One Thought

Father, it's easy for us or for our
child to feel disliked or even hated.
How comforting to know that you
understand. We forget that your son
was hated. Please comfort _____ today
with the thought that you understand.

One Word

CHOSE

One Verse

"You did not choose me, but I chose you
and appointed you that you should go and
bear fruit and that your fruit should abide,
so that whatever you ask the Father in my
name, he may give it to you."

~ John 15:16

One Thought

Father, thank you for choosing me!
What joy it can bring to my heart (and
to my child's heart) to walk through
this day with the thought, *You chose me!*

One Word

DAILY

ONE VERSE

"Blessed be the Lord, who daily bears
us up; God is our salvation."

~ Psalm 68:19

ONE THOUGHT

Father, I spend too much time with concerns about the future. I forget that you are my daily (yes hourly and every minute) Savior. Jesus told us to pray for you to give us *daily* bread. Help me to focus on this day, and accept your provision for this moment.

One Word

WILL

ONE VERSE

"For it is God who works in you, both to will and to work for his good pleasure."

~ Philippians 2:13

ONE THOUGHT

Lord, I don't know which way to go, but you are in charge of my will when I submit to you. Nudge my "willer" so that it is in line with your will and so that your way is accomplished.

One Word

RESTORE

ONE VERSE

"Restore to me the joy of your salvation,
and uphold me with a willing spirit."

~ Psalm 51:12

ONE THOUGHT

Father, sometimes I lose my joy—even
in knowing you. But you are the God
who loves to restore! Please restore me,
restore _____ today with the simple joy
that we get to know you. May this be
enough.

One Word

AWESOME

One Verse

"By awesome deeds
you answer us with righteousness,
O God of our salvation,
the hope of all the ends of the earth
and of the farthest seas."

~ Psalm 65:5

One Thought

Father, I want to dwell today on how awesome you are. When I do this, my issues seem smaller. Please keep me focused on you throughout this day. Help me to memorize this verse and make it real in my life.

One Word

CHOSEN ONE

One Verse

"Behold my servant, whom I uphold,
my chosen, in whom my soul delights;
I have put my Spirit upon him; he will
bring forth justice to the nations."

~ Isaiah 42:1

One Thought

God, you chose Jesus (see also Luke 9:35) as your anointed one. There is no other Savior. We need no other options. You, Jesus, are it. You are enough. Today help me to remember that in every way, you, Jesus, are enough.

One Word

FORTRESS

One Verse

"O my Strength, I will sing praises to
you, for you, O God, are my fortress,
the God who shows me steadfast love."

~ Psalm 59:17

One Thought

Father, I am safe in your fortress. I
can rely on you today. You have me
surrounded.

One Word

STRENGTH

One Verse

"God, the Lord, is my strength;
he makes my feet like the deer's;
he makes me tread on my high places."

~ Habakkuk 3:19

One Thought

Father, I can't do "it"—whatever the it is (forgive someone, ask forgiveness, do a task, have that conversation...) but you, God, are my strength for this. Please enable me to do what you have called me to do.

One Word

WEPT

ONE VERSE

"Jesus wept."

~ John 11:35

ONE THOUGHT

Jesus, it is overwhelming to consider your compassion. You wept over the death of Lazarus even when you knew you were going to raise him. You weep with us and over us and our children. Your tears fall with mine. What soothing tenderness.

One Word

SHOWS

One Verse

"But God shows his love for us in that while
we were still sinners, Christ died for us."

~ Romans 5:8

One Thought

If you, God almighty, would send your
son to die for me in my own wickedness,
then how much more will you show me
how to make the decision I need to make.

One Word

RICH

ONE VERSE

"But God, being rich in mercy, because of the great love with which he loved us, even when we were dead in our trespasses, made us alive together with Christ—by grace you have been saved."

~ Ephesians 2:4

ONE THOUGHT

Father, there is nothing about you that is tight, cheap or thrifty. You are RICH with me. I ask that today I, my child, my friend - would think on the ramifications of this trait of yours...rich in mercy towards me.

One Word

ALL COMFORT

ONE VERSE

"Blessed be the God and Father of our
Lord Jesus Christ, the Father of mercies
and God of all comfort, who comforts
us in all our affliction."

~ 2 Corinthians 1:3-4

ONE THOUGHT

Father, please comfort _____ today. Give
them a very personal awareness of your
supernatural comfort. Touch them in a
way that you know will enable them to
experience it.

One Word

FILLS

One Verse

"May the God of hope fill you with all joy and peace in believing, so that by the power of the Holy Spirit you may abound in hope."

~ Romans 15:13

One Thought

God, today I need some "filling." Thank you that you love to fill your children. Please fill _____ with hope. Teenagers especially need hope. Please fill _____ today with hope.

One Word

RIGHTEOUSNESS

One Verse

"Righteous are you, O Lord,
and right are your rules."

~ Psalm 119:137

One Thought

Father, you alone are right, pure, holy and just. No human is, even though through your cross we are seen as righteous. When I see the dirt in my soul and in the world it is helpful to know that there is one completely pure—you. I want to cling to your purity today. Your righteousness gives me perspective; it encourages hope.

One Word

CARES

One Verse

"...casting all your anxieties on him,
because he cares for you."

~ 1 Peter 5:7

One Thought

Father, there are so many things I can
be anxious about today. Instead of
"mental churning" help me to choose to
say throughout the day, "Right at this
moment you are caring for me, caring
for _____.

One Word

GENTLE

One Verse

"Come to me, all who labor and are
heavy laden, and I will give you rest.
Take my yoke upon you, and learn from
me, for I am gentle and lowly in heart,
and you will find rest for your souls."

~ Matthew 11:28-29

One Thought

Jesus, pour your gentle and humble
spirit into my heart today. My tendency
is to be critical. Remove my critical spirit
for _____ and replace it with a gentle,
humble heart of love for this person.

One Word

BROKEN

One Verse

"And he took bread, and when he had given
thanks, he broke it and gave it to them,
saying, 'This is my body, which is given for
you. Do this in remembrance of me."

~ Luke 22:19

One Thought

There is so much brokenness in our
world. I am broken. So is _____. One
thing all humans have in common is our
brokenness. Jesus, you are intimately
familiar with brokenness. Your body
was broken for me, for _____. You
understand the pain of brokenness but it
is in your brokenness that we can begin
to experience wholeness.

One Word

NOT FAILED

One Verse

"Blessed be the Lord who has given rest to his people Israel, according to all that he promised. Not one word has failed of all his good promise, which he spoke by Moses his servant."

~ 1 Kings 8:56

One Thought

God, I fail, over and over. Others fail me and fail my children. But you, oh Lord, will never fail us. Help me to think on the thought, *Your promises never fail,* throughout this day. I *can* count on you.

One Word

MIGHTY

ONE VERSE

"O Lord God of hosts, who is mighty
as you are, O Lord,
with your faithfulness all around you?"

~ Psalm 89:8

ONE THOUGHT

Father, too often I forget that you are mighty. I unknowingly assign to you my own weakness without even realizing it. Forgive me. I want to dwell on your mighty power today. Your might that levels mountains, raises seas, heals diseases, changes hearts and creates a complex human body. When I focus on your might my perspective is restored.

One Word

ABOUNDING

One Verse

"For you, O Lord, are good and
forgiving, abounding in steadfast love
to all who call upon you."

~ Psalm 86:5

One Thought

Father, your love is abounding, pouring
out, so much more than I can imagine. It
is not parceled out or skimpy. It is more
than I could ever need. It is enough.

One Word

BRINGS UP

One Verse

"I went down to the land whose bars
closed upon me forever;
yet you brought up my life from the pit,
O Lord my God."

~ Jonah 2:6

One Thought

God, there is no pit that is too deep that
you won't lift me out. You bring us up
dear Father. Please bring _____ out of
the pit. Jonah's phrase *yet you...* is full
of hope today.

One Word

SPIRIT OF
TRUTH

ONE VERSE

"And I will ask the Father, and he will give you another Helper, to be with you forever, even the Spirit of truth."

~ John 14:16-17

ONE THOUGHT

In a world of so much that is not true, Jesus you have given us a Counselor, the Spirit of Truth. I can be confident that this Holy Spirit will continue to reveal truth to me. I don't need to be confused. There is one truth and you are it.

One Word

EVERLASTING ARMS

ONE VERSE

"The eternal God is your dwelling
place, and underneath are the
everlasting arms. And he thrust out the
enemy before you and said, 'Destroy'."

~ Deuteronomy 33:27

ONE THOUGHT

God, I love it that you gave your
children simple pictures to understand
complicated truths. Thank you for your
everlasting arms that are under me,
under _____ right at this moment. Place
this picture in the front of my mind as I
live this day.

BEGINNINGS

Most books end with a conclusion. This signifies a finish, a completion. But this devotional is different. My hope is that this small book will serve as a "kick-starter" for you. I pray that you will be inspired to write your own 100 one words. Let the Holy Spirit speak to your heart, reminding you of things He has taught you. Ask Him to reveal to you each day one character trait of our mighty God, that your heart would be turned to Him and you would be filled with the joy of being in His presence throughout your day.

You make known to me the path of life;
In your presence there is fullness of
joy; at your right hand are pleasures
forevermore.

~ Psalm 16:11

A perfect companion book for *One Devotional.*

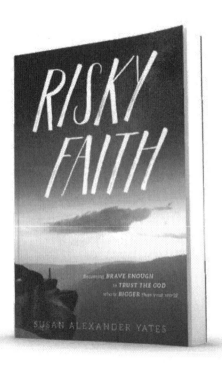

Risky Faith from Susan Alexander Yates
is excellent for both personal use
and small group study.

More Books from
Susan Alexander Yates

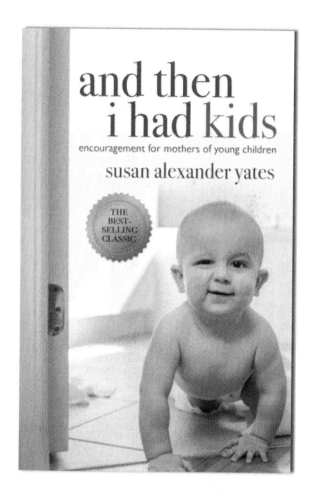

CHARACTER MATTERS:

Raising Kids
With
Values
That
Last

JOHN AND SUSAN YATES

Made in the USA
Lexington, KY
06 September 2019